2

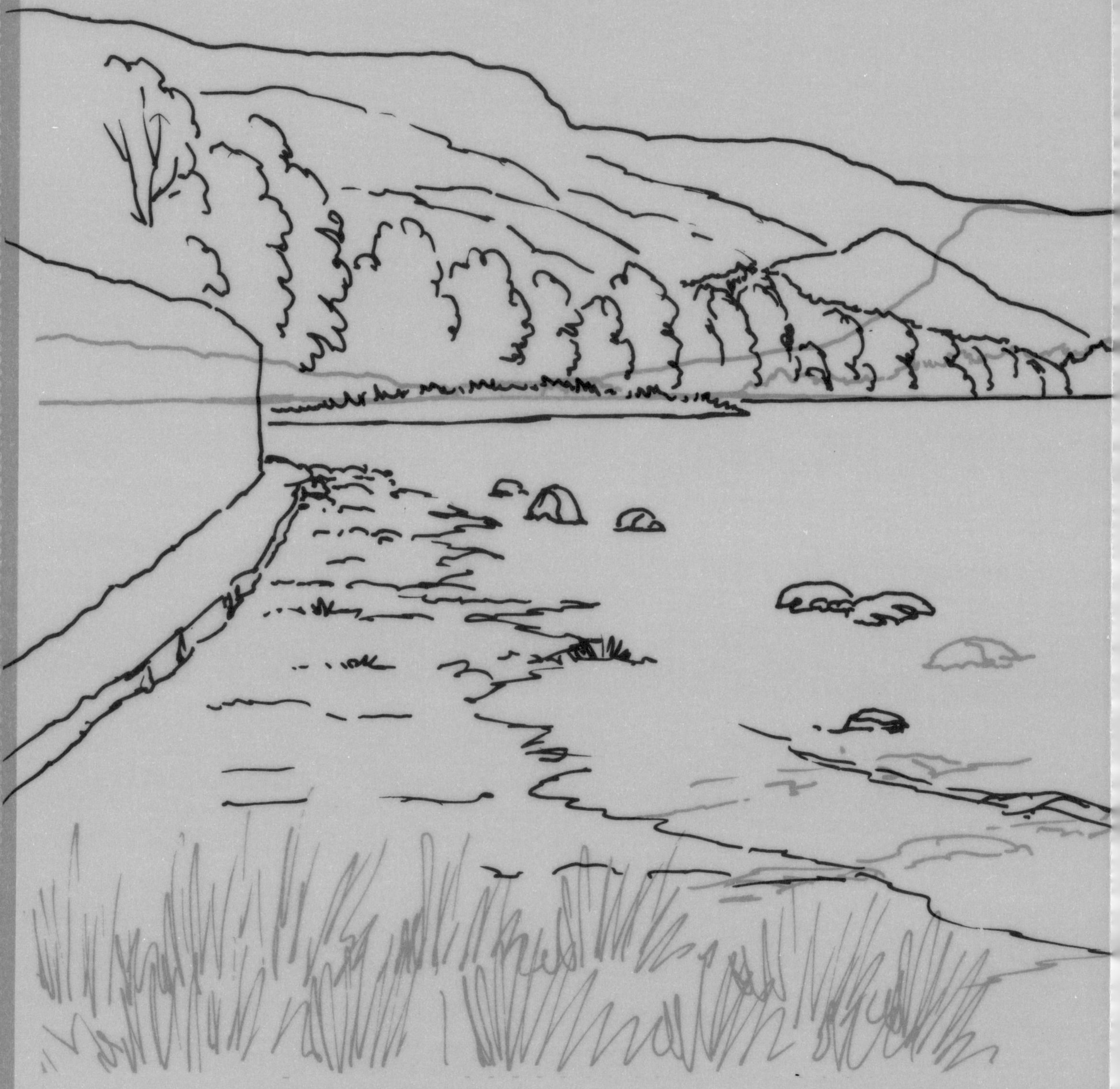

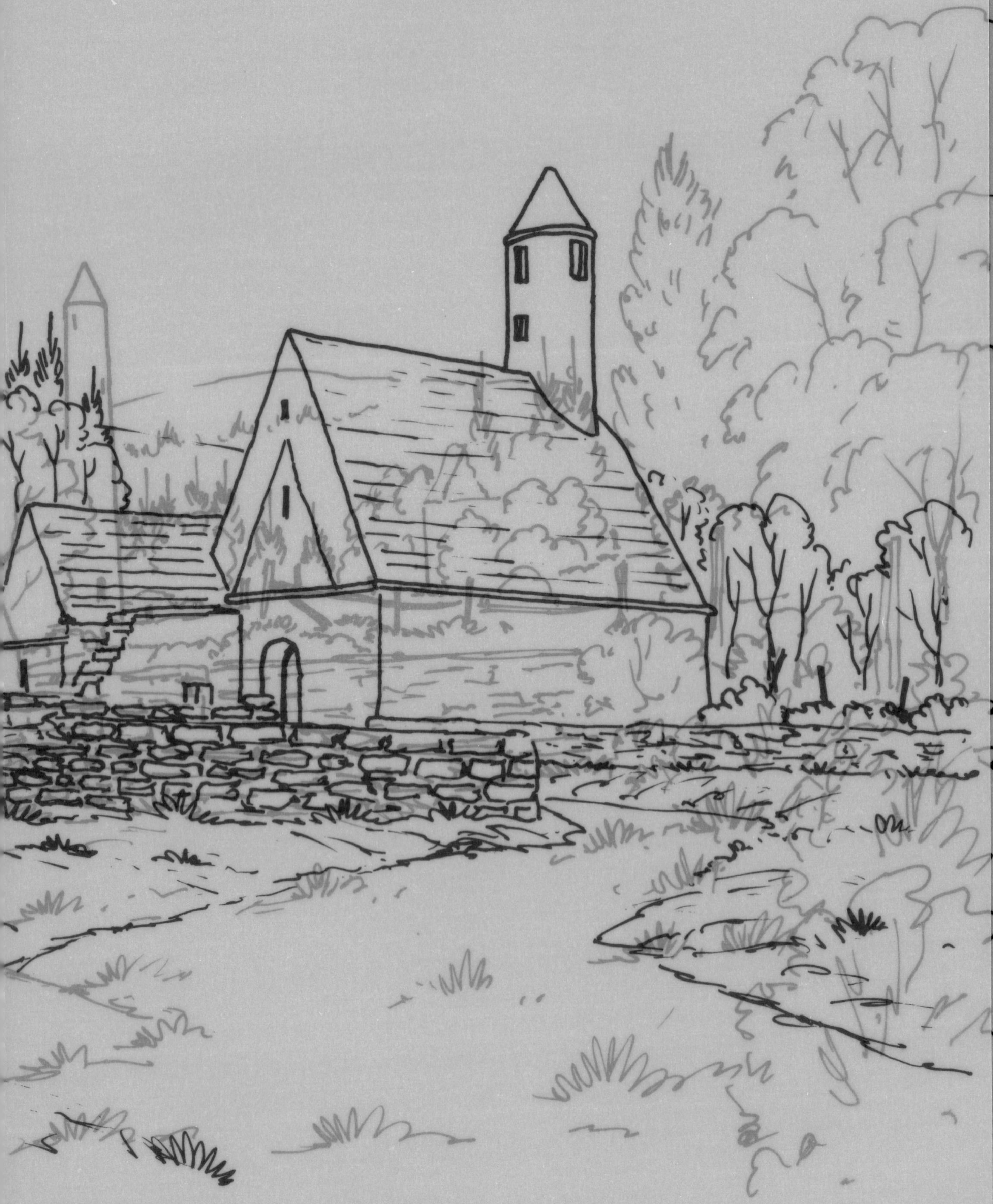

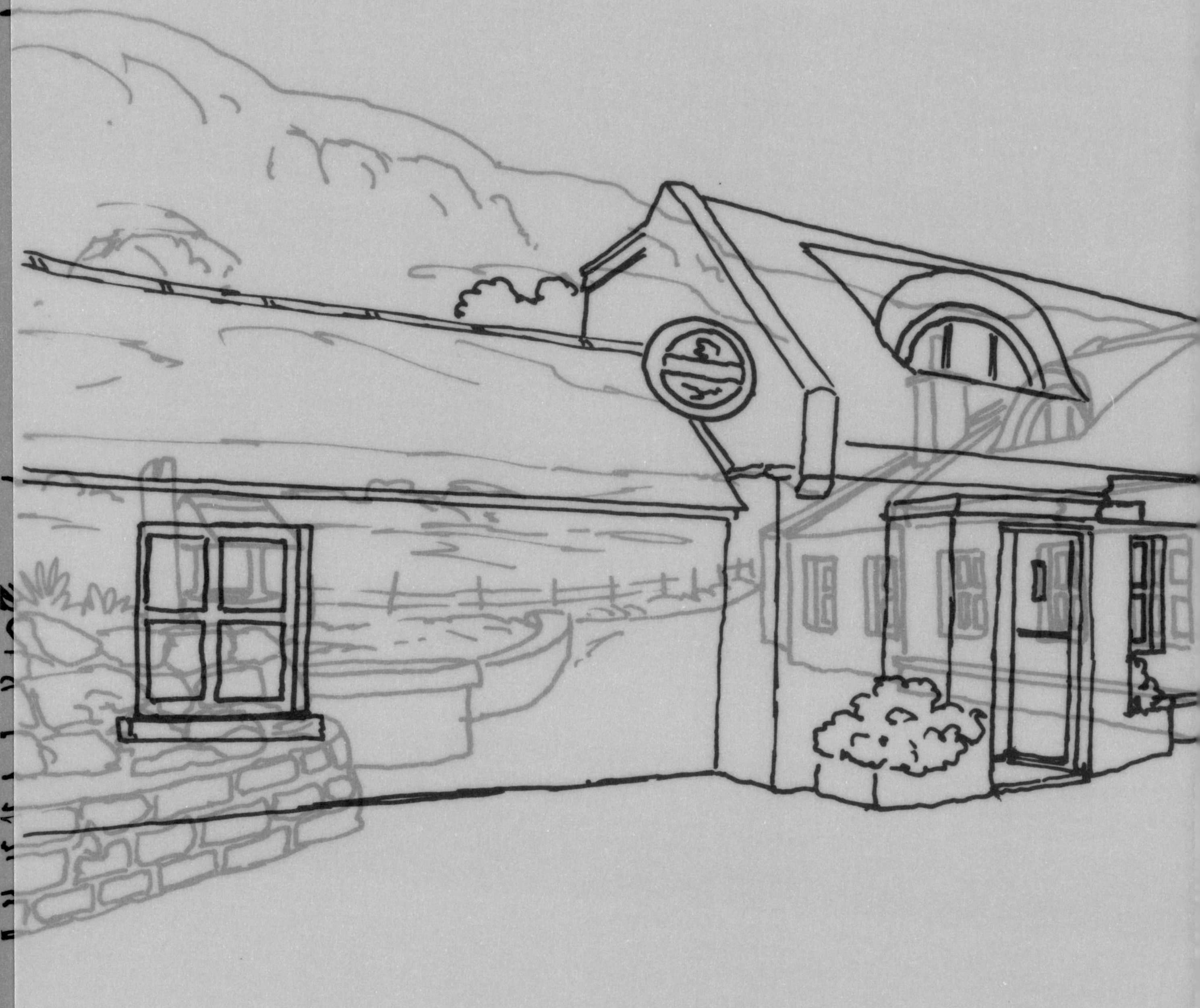

READY TO PAINT

Irish Landscapes
in Watercolour

Dermot Cavanagh

GILL & MACMILLAN

Published in Ireland in 2014 by
Gill & Macmillan
Hume Avenue, Park West, Dublin 12
with associated companies throughout the world
www.gillmacmillanbooks.ie

ISBN 978 0 7171 6034 1

Suppliers
If you have any difficulty obtaining any of the materials and equipment mentioned in this book, please visit the Search Press website: www.searchpress.com

Publisher's notes
All the step-by-step photographs in this book feature the author, Dermot Cavanagh, demonstrating watercolour painting techniques. No models have been used.

Please note that when removing the perforated sheets of tracing paper from the book, score them first, then carefully pull out each sheet.

Printed in China

Dedication
To my family and friends, fellow painters and to all who share my love of painting.

Acknowledgements
I should like to acknowledge the professionalism and help from my editor, Sophie Kersey, and photographer, Paul Bricknell, both of whom made the step-by-step studio experience so enjoyable. I would also like to thank Stena Line for helping with my travel arrangements from my home in Ireland to the Search Press Studios. As ever I thank my wife, Maria, for her continuous encouragement and support.

Page 1
Carlingford
40.5 x 30.5cm (16 x 12in)

Carlingford is a very picturesque coastal town in northern County Louth; it is situated between Carlingford Lough and Slieve Foy, sometimes known as Carlingford Mountain. The mountain dominates most views of the small town. Also in this composition I have included the historic stone-built gatehouse and the remains of the medieval town wall. For the mountains, I used four washes of varying strengths: for the lightest sunlit green, Winsor yellow and a little cobalt turquoise (light); for the darker green, Winsor yellow and Winsor blue; for the earthiness, raw sienna and light red and for the darker top, French ultramarine and light red. These were all painted wet into wet and then blended with a dry 19mm (¾in) flat brush in the direction of the fall.

Opposite
Arranmore Island, County Donegal
40.5 x 30.5cm (16 x 12in)

Arranmore is the largest inhabited island of County Donegal and the second largest in all of Ireland. Its population of approximately 500 people live mostly in the southeast where the coastline is adorned with a necklace of white sandy beaches. This painting was done on the most westerly of the beaches where the old pier looks back towards the Donegal mainland. I pulled Jimmy Bonner's boat into this position and arranged the red box, the oil drum and the lobster pot to improve the foreground composition. Everything else is quite natural.

Contents

Introduction

Learning to paint can be frustrating, and many give up before they really get started, but don't be put off – help is at hand. With good guidance it can be made easier, the frustration can be banished and with a few simple hints and tips, painting can become a very rewarding activity. There are three things that will make you a better painter: observation, self confidence and practice.

Some people say that practice makes perfect, but I say this is only true if you are practising techniques that will actually work! Using this book as your guide, you will learn how to paint what you see and not what you think you see. You do not need to draw the scenes, as they are provided as pull-out tracings that you can transfer on to your watercolour paper, and the step-by-step instructions will take you through the colour mixing and painting techniques. Then with a little practice and growing confidence, successful watercolour paintings will soon follow.

I have chosen a variety of inspirational Irish landscapes for this book, and each of the scenes holds a special significance for me. I have also tried to cover many different themes, such as buildings in the landscape, skies and foregrounds, mountains and lakes, trees and foliage, stone and brickwork, light and shade and aerial perspective.

As you will discover, I use very few materials: twelve colours, five brushes and only a few other accessories. I don't believe in over-complicating the subject. I always try to use the unique clarity and transparency of the watercolour medium to its best effect. I recommend while working through this book that you try to preserve the wonderful qualities of artists' watercolour by avoiding over-working your paintings; let the paints and the paper work for you.

Good luck, have fun, and don't worry about making a few mistakes; you never know, some might even work in your favour.

TRACING

6

Castle Island

40.5 x 30.5cm (16 x 12in)

Castle Island is in Lough Key, County Roscommon and is part of the Shannon–Erne Waterway, a navigable canal linking the River Shannon in the Republic of Ireland with the River Erne in Northern Ireland. This simple but effective painting captures the mystic atmosphere of the place. It is clearly a cold day, but the painting has plenty of warmth. To create this I used a very dilute mixture of light red and crimson in the lower half of the sky, the foreground water and snow washes. I used warm washes of raw sienna and raw sienna and light red on the castle walls. The green and rusty red washes I bled into the background trees have also added warmth. This is all contrasted by the cool bluish washes. The pale blue in the sky is a dilute wash of cerulean and Winsor blue while the clouds are a slightly stronger mixture of cerulean blue and a little neutral tint bled in and blended while the sky was still wet. The background trees are varying strength washes of French ultramarine and a light red, painted wet into wet. The sunlit tree trunks were scratched out with a penknife just before the washes dried.

Materials

Paints

I use Artist quality watercolours in tube form. They are a little bit more expensive than Student quality but the results are well worth the extra cost. I replenish the paint wells of my large studio paint box from twelve specially selected tubes of Winsor & Newton Artist's Watercolour: Winsor yellow, raw sienna, light red, French ultramarine, cerulean blue, Winsor blue (red shade), burnt sienna, neutral tint, alizarin crimson, cobalt turquoise (light), Winsor red and Winsor violet (dioxazine). The intermixing of these twelve colours allows me to create any painting anywhere in the world. Sometimes I use a little titanium white when it is impossible to paint around a window frame, as in the Argory project (page 10). The wings of my paint box open into a large palette, offering lots of mixing space, and they can easily be removed for cleaning. When replenishing from the tubes, I recommend that you simply squeeze your tube colours into the pans until filled flush with the top of the pan. Then leave the box standing open until the paint hardens. This is more economical, as you tend to use more paint than you need if it is wet.

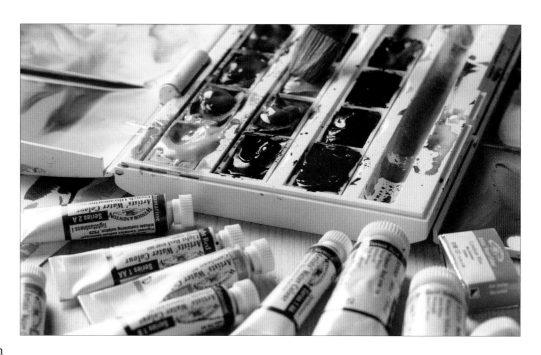

Paper

Choosing which paper to use can be very confusing; there are so many thicknesses, sizes and surface textures. When looking at paper surfaces, Hot Pressed means smooth, Cold Pressed or Not means a medium texture and Rough is of course rough. The thickness or weight of paper is denoted by its gsm (grams per square metre) or lb in imperial. Throughout my career I have experienced most of what is available, with the result that I only use the highest quality watercolour paper for my landscape paintings. As a rule I use Saunders Waterford paper; 300gsm (140lb) Rough surface for paintings of quarter imperial or up to A3 size and heavier weight 640gsm (300lb) Rough for paintings larger than A3 or up to full imperial size. The Rough surface texture has lots of natural peaks and troughs for the watercolour pigment to collect in. Rough paper is fantastic for landscape paintings where the rugged nature of the surface enhances the textures of the painting.

Brushes

I use very few brushes, only five really. Over the years I have always recommended excellent quality at an affordable price. My five brushes allowed me to accomplish all of the painting techniques set out in this book and indeed most of the watercolour paintings I have ever done. The two red-handled brushes are Winsor and Newton Sceptre Gold, a 19mm (¾in) flat and a no. 8 round sable/synthetic blend. The synthetic content gives the brush a good spring, while the sable hair allows great water retention. The two smaller dark blue-handled brushes are Winsor and Newton Artist's Watercolour Sable, a no. 5 round and a no. 2 rigger. Normally, sable brushes are very expensive but these brushes have been produced to a very high standard at great value for money. The light blue synthetic brush is one I made myself during a visit to the Crown Art Brush factory in Lowestoft, Norfolk. I wanted a brush that would allow the students at my art courses to paint foreground grass quickly and successfully. Since then I have found even more uses for it, one of which is removing mistakes.

The rigger, no. 5 round, no. 8 round, 19mm (¾in) flat and synthetic oil painting brush.

Other materials

I made my **drawing board** from 13mm (½in) thick MDF measuring 51 x 40.5cm (20 x 16in). The watercolour paper is then taped to the board along all four edges using a 2.5cm (1in) wide roll of **masking tape**.

My **water container** is a yellow plastic beach bucket. This bucket was used by many celebrities during the filming of my BBC TV series *Awash with Colour*.

I recommend you use a **soft graphite stick** for shading the back of the tracing. Solid graphite sticks such as the one in the picture last for a very long time, allowing you to do many sketches. Use a hard **Conté pencil** for tracing through the sketch. A hard lead will keep its point and can then be used for strengthening the sketch if needed after tracing.

I use a roll of **kitchen paper** for drying my brushes before blending washes, for lifting out colour and to help remove any errors.

I use a **putty eraser** to clean off any graphite smudging from the paper before painting.

I always sign my paintings with a pigmented black ink 0.5 **drawing pen**. It is also very useful if you need to include any emphasising lines in your finished painting. Pigmented ink is permanent, waterproof and lightfast, so it will not fade.

I use a **penknife** for scratching out during the painting and a little **plastic pipette** for wetting any paints that have hardened in the palette if I have left them sitting for a period of time. I also use a little cutting of watercolour paper to test my colour mixes during the painting.

Transferring the image

Tracings are provided at the front of this book for all the step-by-step projects, and for the painting on pages 4–5. Pull out the tracing you want, follow the steps below and transferring the image to your watercolour paper could not be easier. You can re-use the tracing several times without having to re-coat with graphite.

1 Carefully pull out a tracing from the front of the book and rub the back of each line of the image with a 6B graphite stick.

2 Secure a sheet of watercolour paper to your drawing board and place the tracing squarely on top, right side up, using a strip of masking tape to hold it in place. Go over the lines with a hard pencil.

3 Lift up the tracing as you go to check that the image has transferred on to the watercolour paper.

9

The Argory

I run regular painting courses at this magnificent National Trust property near Moy in Northern Ireland. It is a stunning location offering an endless variety of painting opportunities. Built in the 1820s, the Argory is an Irish gentry house offering sweeping vistas over the River Blackwater, scenic woodland and a courtyard and barns. I have a studio in the octagon room of the west wing. For this exercise I painted the front and east-facing façade of the house, treating a complicated scene very simply. The sunlit house front creates an effective contrast with the shadows on the east-facing walls. The house is nicely framed by the dark trees to either side.

You will need

300gsm (140lb) Rough watercolour paper

Colours: Winsor blue, cerulean blue, Winsor yellow, cobalt turquoise, French ultramarine, light red, alizarin crimson, raw sienna, Winsor violet, Winsor red, titanium white, neutral tint

Brushes: 19mm (¾in) flat, no. 8 round, no. 5 round, rigger

Kitchen paper, penknife

1 Using the 19mm (¾in) flat brush, mix four brushfuls of water with Winsor blue and a little cerulean blue. Wet the paper, going down over the trees but cutting neatly around the chimneys and roof. Make horizontal strokes with the wash, full strength at the top and fading lower down.

2 Make three washes for the foreground grass: a light acid green from three brushfuls of water with Winsor yellow and a little cobalt turquoise; a dark green from one brushful of water with Winsor yellow and French ultramarine; and one brushful of water with light red, very dilute. Wet the largest area of lawn evenly then apply the first wash with horizonal strokes.

3 Nip the brush dry between your finger and thumb with kitchen paper, pick up the dark green wash and put in a few horizontal strokes while the first wash is wet. The second and subsequent washes should always be thicker to avoid backruns. Do the same with the light red wash, suggesting clay or dried grass in the lawn.

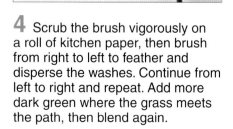

4 Scrub the brush vigorously on a roll of kitchen paper, then brush from right to left to feather and disperse the washes. Continue from left to right and repeat. Add more dark green where the grass meets the path, then blend again.

5 Paint the other smaller sections of lawn with the same three washes, but without applying water first. Emphasise the edges of the path with the darker green wash, and blend as before.

6 Make a wash of raw sienna, cerulean blue and Winsor red and keep mixing in the palette as the colours granulate. Use the no. 8 brush to paint the main facade, keeping the leading edge of the paint wet so no hard lines develop.

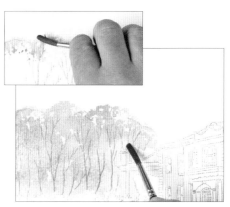

7 Keep the colours well mixed in the palette and paint the gable end wall. Paint in small sections, edging downwards and keeping the leading edge wet, like the tide coming in. The downpipe and creepers divide the wall into sections, which helps.

8 Paint the octagon room to the left of the building in the same way. The central porch is made from lighter, finely cut limestone so the wash should be more diluted. Add chimneys and other details, including the window reveals.

9 Mix three brushfuls of water with French ultramarine and a little light red. Take the brush in a flat hold, parallel to the paper surface and pull it across the surface to create the broken outline of the hazy distant trees. Block in the rest, cutting round the house details.

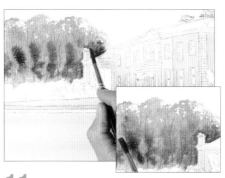

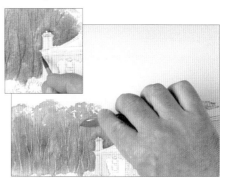

10 While this wash is damp, bleed in the thicker, darker lawn mix of Winsor yellow and French ultramarine from two-thirds of the way up, down to the bottom.

11 While this is damp, pick up a thicker wash of French ultramarine and a bit of light red and make downward strokes a little apart for the deeper shadows. Concentrate this dark mix around the house. Nip the brush dry as before and diffuse the dark marks into the wash.

12 Use the smaller no. 5 brush and the dark tree mix to paint negatively round the details of the chimney pot, coping stone and lead flashing of the roof. Take a penknife and while the tree area is just damp, scratch out sunlit trunks and branches.

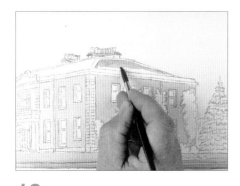

13 For the roof, take the no. 8 brush and mix two brushfuls of water with cerulean blue and alizarin crimson. This will separate, so keep mixing it. It will then granulate on the paper to create a good texture.

14 Paint the distant trees to the right of the house in the same way as those on the left, and scratch out trunks and branches with the penknife as before.

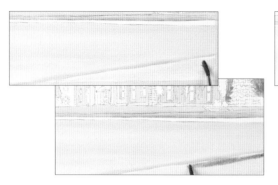

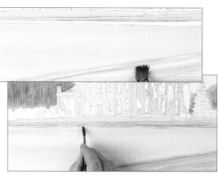

15 Mix two no. 8 brushfuls of water with raw sienna and a little neutral tint and paint the path at the bottom of the picture. Brush in a thicker mix of raw sienna and Winsor violet along the edge while the first wash is wet.

16 Use a dried 19mm (¾in) flat brush to blend in the darker mix, creating texture. Paint the distant path in the same way, but using the no. 8 brush.

17 Make three washes for the bushes beneath the distant trees: Winsor yellow with cobalt turquoise; Winsor yellow and French ultramarine and French ultramarine and light red. Paint the first wash into the bushes, cutting round the palms.

18 Bleed in shadows on the right and undersides of the bushes with the darker wash.

19 Paint in the third wash for the extreme darks, cutting round the palms.

20 Use the same three mixes to paint the creepers on the house walls, painting in the light yellow mix first. Dot in a little of the medium green mix, then nip the brush dry and blend and diffuse the colours.

21 Dot in and blend the darkest wash in the same way, and continue with all the creeper covering the house.

22 For the conifer on the right, mix two brushfuls of water with French ultramarine and Winsor yellow with a bit of light red. Use the point of the no. 8 brush to paint the clumps of foliage, from the top down. Halfway down, bleed in a stronger mix of the same colours. Continue, alternating the strengths.

23 Paint the palms on the left with the Winsor yellow and cobalt turquoise mix.

24 Make a very dilute mix of cerulean blue and alizarin crimson and paint the lead flashing on the roof. Change to the no. 5 brush and paint the chimney pots with light red.

25 Use the no. 8 brush to make a shadow mix of French ultramarine, a tiny bit of light red and a tiny bit of Winsor red. Use this to add shadow to the stonework of the house, starting with the gable end wall. Do not shade the creeper. Cut carefully round the windows and remember to shade the reveals.

26 Make a stronger shadow mix with more French ultramarine and light red, and use the no. 5 brush to block in the windows. Use the same dark mix to shadow under the eaves and the lead flashing.

27 Paint the dark details of the door and porch with the same mix.

28 Fill in any gaps in the foliage to the left of the house with Winsor yellow, and paint the terracotta pot with light red.

29 Use a rigger brush and titanium white to paint the white of the window frames.

30 Add life to the picture by painting birds in the sky, using the rigger and a mix of darks from your palette.

Overleaf

The finished painting.

13

DERMOT CAVANAGH.

Glencar Lake

This lovely lough is in a deep valley north of Sligo town and just south-east of Benbulben mountain. This is one of the locations I used during my BBC TV series *Awash with Colour*. My painting guest was former pop singer and TV presenter, Toyah Wilcox. From this viewpoint, looking west along the lough from a nearby road, the scene is a perfect composition for a painting. The horizon is slightly below half-way down and the bulk of the mountain is off-centre and to the right. The right-hand foreground leads you in, and the dark grass gives balance to the left-hand side. The lough shore, the wall in the bottom left, the line of green trees in the middle distance and the mountain all create linear perspective, with the lines sloping away as they recede, and the blue distance creates aerial perspective.

You will need

300gsm (140lb) Rough watercolour paper

Colours: Winsor blue, cerulean blue, light red, neutral tint, raw sienna, Winsor yellow, French ultramarine, Winsor blue

Brushes: 19mm (¾in) flat, no. 8 round, no. 5 round, old nylon brush, rigger

Kitchen paper, penknife

1 Use the 19mm (¾in) flat brush to make three sky washes: four brushfuls of water with Winsor blue and cerulean blue; three brushfuls of water with light red; and two brushfuls of water with cerulean blue and neutral tint. Evenly wet the paper from the top down with clean water, in horizontal strokes, down to the waterline. Bleed in the light red wash, creating blustery shapes.

2 Paint the sky blue in from the top left-hand corner, leaving white space for cloud shapes, then use what is left on the brush to create an underbelly for the clouds.

3 Scrub the brush dry vigorously on kitchen paper, then use it to mop up any unwanted streaks or runs in the sky and to blend and diffuse the colours while the washes are wet.

4 Still working into the damp background, add darker clouds with the third, thickest wash. Make them smaller at the bottom to create perspective. As before, scrub the brush dry and use it to soften and diffuse some clouds, leaving others as they are. Leave to dry.

5 Make washes for the foreground gravel: one with three brushfuls of water with raw sienna and a touch of neutral tint and a second thicker, darker wash of raw sienna, light red and a little neutral tint. Pre-wet the area evenly with clean water and bleed in the first wash.

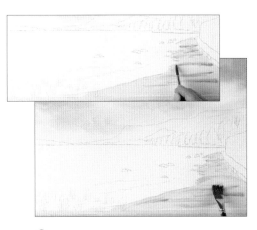

6 Use the no. 8 round brush to bleed in the second wash, with lines following the contour of the land. Change to a dry 19mm (¾in) flat brush to blend and diffuse these marks.

7 While this is damp, mix a green from Winsor yellow and a tiny bit of French ultramarine, and apply a little of this with the point of the no. 8 brush. Again, blend with a dry 19mm (¾in) brush, and allow the painting to dry.

8 Apply the same first wash of raw sienna and a touch of neutral tint to the wall on the right, then paint vertical strokes of the second wash into this, to show the direction in which water staining effects the wall. Scrub dry the brush and blend. Apply the green mix in the same way and blend as before.

9 Paint the pathway beneath the wall in the same way, but with horizontal strokes as shown. Run a little of the colour along the edge to remove the white, and allow to dry.

10 Make three washes for the mountains using the no. 8 brush: three brushfuls of water with French ultramarine and a little light red for a greyish blue; two brushfuls of water with Winsor yellow and a little French ultramarine for a mid-tone green; and two brushfuls of water with lots of French ultramarine and light red, to make a grey-navy. Wet the mountain area, but not up to the pencil mark. This retards the drying time without creating a hard line. Paint the first wash from the top of the mountain to define the edge, and block in below.

11 While this is damp, apply the green wash two-thirds of the way up. Nip the brush dry with kitchen paper between your thumb and finger, and diffuse the green into the blue.

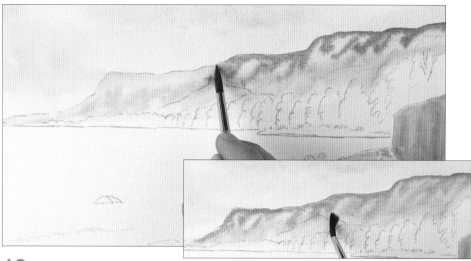

12 Paint the third, dark wash from the top of the mountains and pull a few 'legs' down into the green. Scrub the brush dry on kitchen paper and use it to diffuse and blend the marks.

13 Add a few more ruts and crevices with the same mix and blend and diffuse them as before. While the area is damp, emphasise the top edge of the mountains and blend with a dry brush. Allow to dry.

14 To paint the distant trees on the left, mix two brushfuls of water with French ultramarine, a little Winsor yellow and a tiny bit of light red. Use the tip of the no. 8 brush to paint the top of the area, then feed in a darker mix of French ultramarine and light red down to the waterline, and let this bleed up.

15 Paint the distant trees below the main peak in the same way, using the first wash to suggest the top shapes of conifers, then painting the darker wash at the waterline and allowing it to bleed up. Repeat to the left of this area in the far distance.

16 Make three washes for the sunlit area of trees: three brushfuls of water with Winsor yellow and a little Winsor blue; two brushfuls with lots of Winsor yellow, lots of French ultramarine and a little light red to make a dark green; and two brushfuls with French ultramarine and light red for the darkest tones. Block in the first stretch of the sunlit trees with the first acid green wash.

17 While the first wash is wet, shade the left-hand side and underside of each tree with the second dark green wash.

18 Bleed in the third, darkest wash at the extreme left-hand side and underside of the trees, to create further depth to the foliage. Dry the brush on kitchen paper and use the point to blend and soften the tones, bouncing between the darks and lights.

19 Paint the trees to the right of this area in exactly the same way, with the same sequence of three washes, then blend the tones as before.

20 While this area is just damp but not too wet, use a penknife to scratch out trunks and branches catching the light.

21 Wet then shade the peak of distant forest behind these trees with French ultramarine and light red.

22 Dot in texture with a thicker mix of the same colours, then dry the brush and blend.

23 Block in the tree on the far right with Winsor yellow, a tiny bit of raw sienna and Winsor blue. Leave parts of the tree to the left of it showing through.

24 Make a darker, thicker green from Winsor yellow, French ultramarine and light red. Check if it bleeds just enough by painting a face in the first wash and seeing how far it spreads. Then dot in the darks, and diffuse them with a dry brush.

25 Make a dark mix of French ultramarine and light red and bleed this in to create the darkest tones. When the paint is just damp, scratch out trunks and branches with a penknife.

26 Paint the reed bed beneath the trees with the no. 8 brush and dilute raw sienna. Make a darker wash from French ultramarine, light red and a little Winsor yellow and paint a line at the water's edge. Dry the brush and tap the darker paint to prevent it from spreading too far.

27 Make two washes for the water with the 19mm (¾in) flat brush: four brushfuls of water with cerulean blue with a little neutral tint; and two brushfuls with stronger cerulean blue and more neutral tint. Wet the paper evenly, cutting round the foreground rocks. Apply the first wash, leaving a tiny white line at the top.

28 Sweep horizontal lines of the second wash across the water to show texture and movement. Dry the brush and blend these marks in, then allow to dry.

29 Make a shadow wash from three no. 8 brushfuls of water, French ultramarine, a bit of light red and Winsor red. Pull down vertical strokes on the wall, leaving texture. Add shade to the path with horizontal strokes.

30 Make a stronger mix with more French ultramarine and light red and shade the left-hand edge of the path with vertical strokes. Blend with a little water to make this less harsh.

31 Mix raw sienna, neutral tint and a little light red and paint dots and dashes to texture the gravel in the foreground.

32 Make looser and wider marks coming forwards, following the contour of the ground, then blend with an almost dry 19mm (¾in) flat brush.

33 Mix raw sienna and neutral tint with a brushful of water and paint this over the rocks.

34 Use the no. 5 round brush to paint a dark mix of French ultramarine and light red on the left-hand sides of the rocks to give them form.

35 Use the dark tree mix of Winsor yellow, French ultramarine and light red, and the no. 5 brush to flick up grasses in the gravel, placing blades from eleven o'clock through to one o'clock.

36 Take an old nylon or hog hair brush and mix Winsor yellow, lots of French ultramarine and a little light red. Splay the brush and flick up reeds from the masking tape.

37 Add some taller, straggly reeds with the no. 5 brush so that they do not look too uniform.

38 Mix together the water washes and thin them with more water, then paint ripples in the foreground water.

39 Use the rigger and darks from the palette to paint birds.

Overleaf

The finished painting.

21

DERMOT CAVANAGH

Glendalough

Glendalough's spectacular scenery and rich history make it one of the most visited places in Ireland. Located in the Wicklow Mountains, it was a monastic settlement founded in the 6th century by the hermit monk, St Kevin. My surname, Cavanagh, originates from there; it is an anglicisation of the Gaelic Mac Caomhánach 'son of Caomhán' (or follower of Kevin). I kept the sky very simple, so as not to compete with the busy foreground. The only building material shown is dry stone, with no windows, doors, roof tiles or eaves to add interest. To create form and drama in the buildings, I placed the sun high and to the right, which produces very dark interior shadows.

You will need

300gsm (140lb) Rough watercolour paper

Colours: Winsor blue, cerulean blue, light red, alizarin crimson, Winsor yellow, cobalt turquoise, raw sienna, Winsor red, French ultramarine

Brushes: 19mm (¾in) flat, no. 8 round, no. 5 round, rigger

Kitchen paper, penknife

1 Mix two sky washes with the 19mm (¾in) flat brush: four brushfuls of water with Winsor blue and cerulean blue; and three brushfuls of water with light red and alizarin crimson. Wet the paper evenly, cutting round the roofs, then streak the second wash across lower down the sky.

2 Paint the blue wash from the top of the sky in horizontal strokes, fading it down into the pale red mix. Dry the brush on kitchen paper and soften any hard edges, blending the washes together a little.

3 Make a thicker mix of the blue wash and paint more streaks across the sky while it is still wet, then dry the brush and blend and soften as before.

4 Make washes for the foreground grass: three brushfuls of water with Winsor yellow and a tiny bit of cobalt turquoise; two brushfuls with strong Winsor yellow and lots of French ultramarine; and 1 brushful with a thicker light red. Wet the grass area to the right of the path and paint in the first light green wash.

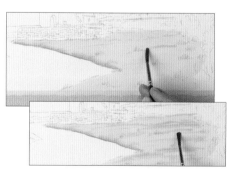

5 Use the no. 8 brush to feed in the dark green at the edges of the grass, and add a few streaks in the body of the grass, falling slightly to the left. Brush in some of the light red wash in the same way to suggest clay or dead grass. Blend and soften with a dry 19mm (¾in) brush. You can add and blend more streaks while the colour is wet.

6 Complete the grassy area on the other side of the path in exactly the same way.

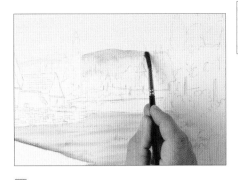

7 Make a grey wash for the distant hills: two brushfuls of water with French ultramarine and a little light red. Wet the area first, but not up to the pencil line, then drop in the wash, outlining the edge. Cut around the trees and houses.

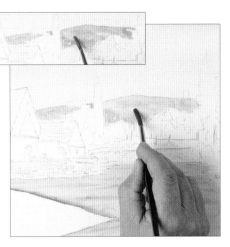

8 Drop in the bright green of the distant grass. Dry the brush and use it to soften and blend the washes.

9 Make washes for the stone roofs: three brushfuls of water, raw sienna and a little cerulean blue; and a thicker mix of two brushfuls with raw sienna, Winsor red and cerulean blue. Block in the roof with the first wash, then bleed in the second in random marks. Nip the brush dry and blend and soften.

10 Continue to paint all the stonework in the same way. Block in the tower with the first wash, then feed in the stronger second wash on the left-hand side. Pull out the bleeding paint towards the middle, then to stop it spreading further, nip the brush dry with kitchen paper and touch the middle area. This creates a cylindrical effect.

11 While the washes are wet, add French ultramarine to the second wash and apply it on the extreme left, then blend out as before.

12 Paint the larger tower on the left in the same way.

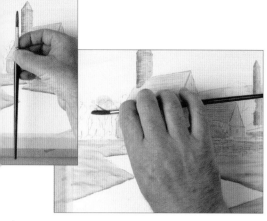

13 Make three washes for the distant trees to the left of the buildings: two brushfuls of water with French ultramarine and light red; two brushfuls with Winsor yellow and French ultramarine; and two brushfuls with stronger French ultramarine and light red. Use a flat hold on the no. 8 brush (see inset) and drag the belly of the brush over the rough paper surface to create a broken outline for the treetops.

14 Block in the rest of the trees in the usual way, cutting round the edges of the building.

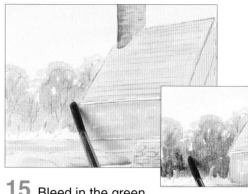

15 Bleed in the green wash two-thirds of the way up. Bleed in the third, dark wash in the bottom half, intensifying it round the light edge of the building and on the left and underside of the foliage.

16 Block in the area of foliage behind the far wall with the light grass wash of Winsor yellow and cobalt turquoise.

17 Use the point of the no. 8 brush to paint the tip of a conifer behind this foliage, using Winsor yellow and French ultramarine. Come in from the left at eleven o'clock, then from the right at one o'clock, and fill in the middle. Continue painting the other conifers in this way. Paint a darker mix on the left-hand sides while the trees are still slightly damp.

18 Paint the yew tree in front of the conifers with the same initial mix, but with a bit more Winsor yellow, then bleed in the darker mix on the left-hand side. Dry the brush and blend it in slightly.

19 For the tree behind the main building, mix two brushfuls of water with Winsor yellow; and Winsor blue with a tiny bit of light red. Brush a bit of water on the bulk of the tree, then paint the broken outline in the yellow, cutting round the roof.

20 Do the happy face test with the second wash to see how far it spreads, and adjust the thickness accordingly, then dot it in, moving out from the centre in a fan shape. Make the dots more concentrated near the building.

21 Mix French ultramarine and light red and dot in the darkest areas near the building. Nip the brush in kitchen paper between your thumb and forefinger and blend and diffuse the washes. Scratch out branches with a penknife.

22 Make a light mix of Winsor yellow and a little Winsor blue for the smaller trees, then bleed in a darker mix of Winsor yellow, Winsor blue and light red. Dry the brush and feather this out into the lighter green. Repeat with the darkest darks, using French ultramarine and light red.

23 Paint the hedge behind the wall in the same way, with the light green first, then the darker mix run in underneath.

24 Darken the main roof with a mix of two brushfuls of water with raw sienna, Winsor red and cerulean blue. Leave flecks of the lighter colour showing through for texture.

25 Continue painting the other roof and all the architectural details in the same way, including under the eaves, the archway and the tower windows.

26 Paint the bushes on the left with the same greens and techniques as the trees.

27 Indicate the stonework on the wall with raw sienna, Winsor red and cerulean blue.

28 Make a very dark mix of French ultramarine and light red and use the no. 5 brush to paint the darkest details: the darks in the windows and the arch and under the eaves.

29 Mix washes for the path: very dilute raw sienna; and Winsor red with cerulean blue. Wet the path first. Paint on the first wash very loosely, in the direction of the path coming forwards.

30 While this is wet, paint a line down the middle of the path with the second wash, then add lines down the right and left and a few more in between. Dry the 19mm (¾in) brush and use it to blend and diffuse the lines.

31 Make washes for the trees on the right: Winsor yellow, raw sienna and French ultramarine; Winsor yellow and lots of French ultramarine to make a dark green; and French ultramarine and light red. Hold the brush flat against the paper and pull the first wash across the surface to create a broken outline of foliage. Continue, changing the direction of the brush.

32 Continue down the tree, leaving sky holes showing through, While this is wet, bleed in the second wash on the underside of the blocks of foliage. Use the third wash for the darkest parts, particularly at the base of the tree, cutting round the fence posts.

33 Use a penknife to scratch out trunks and branches while the paint is just damp. Scratch out the lighter parts of the fence.

34 Mix a shadow wash with the no. 8 brush from three brushfuls of water, French ultramarine and Winsor red. Use this to shadow the darker sides of the buildings, and add the cast shadows.

35 Paint the bushes on the right with the same foliage mixes as before, beginning with Winsor yellow and a little Winsor blue.

36 Bleed in a thicker mix of Winsor yellow and French ultramarine. Work on a few non-adjacent bushes at a time.

37 Continue, adding the darkest wash in the most shadowed parts on the right.

38 Mix light red and raw sienna and fill in between the bushes to vary the tone and colour.

39 Mix some of the green washes and use the point of the no. 8 brush or no. 5 if that is easier, to flick up tufts of grass, growing from eleven o'clock through to one o'clock.

40 Darken and adjust the shadows with a mix of French ultramarine, Winsor red and light red.

41 Use the rigger and darks from the palette to paint birds as a finishing touch.

Overleaf

The finished painting.

DERMOT CAVANAGH

The Singing Pub

The Singing Pub is one of Ireland's great music pubs, situated along the mountain road around the Atlantic Drive on the Rosguill Peninsula. Rosguill has a wealth of painting locations and a few excellent thirst-quenching pubs when you need a break. What I like about the painting is the warm, welcoming atmosphere it portrays, which contrasts well with the shadows, especially the darkness of the window panes. Some people think the windows should reflect the sky colour, but this is only the case with much larger windows.

You will need

300gsm (140lb) Rough watercolour paper

Colours: Winsor blue, cerulean blue, alizarin crimson, neutral tint, raw sienna, French ultramarine, light red, Winsor yellow, Winsor red, cobalt turquoise

Brushes: 19mm (¾in) flat, no. 8 round, no. 5 round, rigger

Kitchen paper

I feel a song coming on – anyone for a pint?

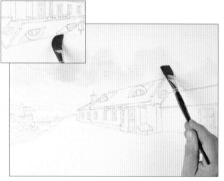

1 Make washes for the sky with the 19mm (¾in) flat brush: four brushfuls of water with Winsor blue and cerulean blue; three brushfuls with alizarin crimson and the blue still on your brush; two brushfuls with cerulean blue and neutral tint. Wet the sky, going over the mountain, but cut round the pub roof by turning the board upside down and using the flat edge of the brush. Brush in swirls of the pinky alizarin crimson wash.

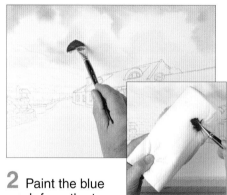

2 Paint the blue wash from the top, leaving white space for clouds, then paint the undersides of the clouds. Scrub the brush dry on kitchen paper and use it to blend streaks and runs and diffuse any shapes that are too definite.

3 Before this dries, paint on the grey cloud wash in patches, then scrub the brush dry again and blend and soften this in. Fade the sky colours downwards so that there will not be a white halo round the buildings.

4 Make washes for the path: four brushfuls of water with raw sienna; two brushfuls with raw sienna and neutral tint; two brushfuls with alizarin crimson and cerulean blue. Wet the paper, then brush in the first wash in the direction of the path.

5 Paint the darker second wash down the middle of the path and at either side, while the first wash is wet.

6 Brush in streaks of the alizarin crimson and cerulean blue mix in the direction of the path. Scrub the brush dry and blend.

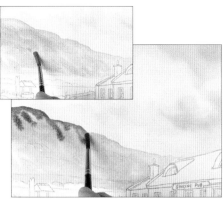
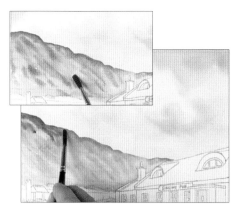

7 Make mountain washes: three no. 8 brushfuls of water with French ultramarine and a little light red; two brushfuls with Winsor yellow and a touch of French ultramarine; two brushfuls with lots of French ultramarine and light red. Wet the mountains with water but not right to the top edge. Cut round the chimney carefully. Use the first wash to define the shape of the mountains.

8 Bleed in the second wash from two-thirds of the way up, cutting round the well. Paint the third wash from the top, pulling it along to define the profile of the mountains, then pull legs down for ruts and crevices.

9 Squeeze the brush dry and nip it into a paddle shape, then use it to smooth and manipulate the colours. While the washes are damp, feed in darker accents on top and blend these in too.

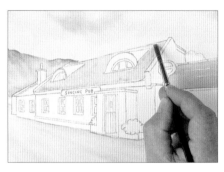

10 Mix two no. 8 brushfuls of water with cerulean blue and a tiny bit of alizarin crimson to make a slate grey and paint this on the right-hand roof, leaving the ridge tiles white. Paint in horizontal lines, leaving a little white to represent the lines of tiles. These colours granulate to create texture.

11 Make washes for the thatched roof: three brushfuls of water with Winsor yellow and raw sienna; raw sienna and light red; and light red and French ultramarine. Wet the roof first, going round the dormer windows and leaving the barges (tops of the gable end walls) dry. Paint in the first yellow wash.

12 Paint lines of the second wash downwards in the direction of the fall of the roof, then paint the third, darkest wash along the bottom edge so that it bleeds up a bit. Again, stroke lines down to suggest weathering. Dry the brush and use it to smooth the effect of the roof and to stop the bleeds.

13 Paint the far roof, which is corrugated tin, with light red and a little Winsor red.

14 Paint the middle distant field with Winsor yellow and French ultramarine.

15 Paint the foliage edge of the tree behind the buildings with a brushful of water mixed with Winsor yellow and French ultramarine. Drop in French ultramarine and light red, dry the brush and blend.

16 Block in the dormer window thatch with the first thatch wash of Winsor yellow and raw sienna, then bleed in the second wash of raw sienna and light red for texture.

17 Edge the dormer window with the darkest wash of light red and French ultramarine, then dry the brush and blend the dark into the lighter tones.

18 Use the no. 5 brush to make washes for the little distant bushes: Winsor yellow and French ultramarine; and French ultramarine and light red. Dry the brush a little and tap in bushes, varying the shapes, then bleed in the darker wash on the right-hand side and undersides. Continue in the same way to the left of the well.

19 Make stone washes: two no. 8 brushfuls of water with raw sienna; and raw sienna, light red and neutral tint. Paint the first wash on the porch, the bleed in texture with the second wash. Nip the brush dry and blend.

20 Paint the porch sides and the lower part of the pub with the same techniques and washes.

21 Make a very dilute mix of raw sienna and cerulean blue for the cement rendering and apply it to the main walls.

22 Paint the annexe with raw sienna and Winsor yellow. While this is wet, bleed in a pink wash of alizarin crimson with cerulean blue, brushing downwards in the direction of water staining.

23 Paint the pub door with the no. 5 brush and a mix of light red and Winsor red. Leave a gap across the middle as it is in two sections. Paint downward strokes to represent the planking.

24 Make two washes for the dry stone wall: dilute raw sienna on its own and raw sienna, light red and cerulean blue. Brush in the two furthest parts of the wall and then introduce the staining with the second wash.

25 Paint a few of the stones in the foreground wall with raw sienna, then bleed the darker wash into the right-hand sides and undersides wet into wet. Work around eight stones at a time. When dry, paint between the stones with the first wash.

26 Make a shadow wash with three no. 8 brushfuls of water with French ultramarine, light red and Winsor red. Add shadow on the gable end wall, the side of the porch, the reveal of the door, under the porch overhang, under the eaves and on the inside of the barge (this is the raised wall edge that protects the roof from wind). Shade under the overhang of the chimney and its right-hand side.

27 Add shadow under any overhanging stonework and under the flowers and the eaves of the tin roof. Paint cast shadows from the walls on the left. Shade the reveals of the windows and add cast shadows from the porch on to the pub wall and from the pub on to the annexe.

28 Make a dark mix of French ultramarine and light red, and use the no. 5 brush to paint the darks in the windows. For the nearer windows, use quick brushstrokes, leaving white sparkles.

29 Use the same wash to emphasise dark details, such as a lost and found edge at the bottom of the roof tiles and under the porch overhang, the dark inside the slightly open porch door and the line between the frame and the door.

30 Shade the door with the shadow wash of French ultramarine, light red and Winsor red.

31 Paint the ridge tiles on the right-hand roof with light red, leaving little vertical bits of white for mortar.

32 Mix Winsor blue and Winsor yellow and paint an impression of the beer sign.

33 Paint the flowers either side of the door with the no. 5 brush and Winsor red, then dot in the foliage with Winsor yelow and cobalt turquoise.

34 Bleed in a dark green on the underside of the foliage with Winsor yellow and French ultramarine.

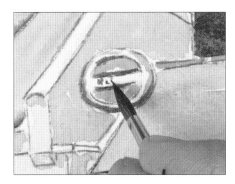

35 Outline the beer sign with the dark wash of French ultramarine and light red, and suggest lettering.

36 Paint the pub sign with the point of the no. 5 brush or the rigger and the same mix.

37 Use the slate roof mix of cerulean blue and alizarin crimson to paint the roof of the well.

38 Paint the terracotta chimney pot with light red.

39 Paint a cast shadow on the annexe roof with the French ultramarine, light red and Winsor red mix.

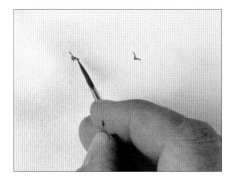

40 Use the rigger and a mix of darks from your palette to paint birds in the sky.

41 Use the green from the beer sign to paint the pub sign background.

42 Finally, paint the fence with the rigger and the window pane wash of French ultramarine and light red.

Overleaf

The finished painting.

37

DERMOT CAVANAGH

Doo Lough

In the heart of Connemara, between the town of Louisburgh and Delphi Lodge, in a wild and unspoilt valley of extraordinary beauty lies the deep and formidable Doo Lough (Black Lake). Overlooked by the tallest mountains in Connemara, the lakes and rivers of the Delphi valley are famous for their salmon and sea trout fishing. The adjective 'awesome' is entirely appropriate. Some would add 'forbidding', while others might say 'majestic'. I filmed three episodes of *Awash with Colour* in this area but never actually got round to painting this scene until now.

I do hope you enjoy it.

You will need

300gsm (140lb) Rough watercolour paper

Colours: Winsor blue, cerulean blue, alizarin crimson, raw sienna, neutral tint, Winsor yellow, cobalt turquoise, French ultramarine, light red, cobalt turquoise, burnt sienna, Winsor red

Brushes: 19mm (¾in) flat, no. 8 round, rigger

Kitchen paper, penknife

1 Make sky washes using the 19mm (¾in) flat brush: two brushfuls of water with Winsor blue and cerulean blue; and two brushfuls with alizarin crimson and the blue left in your brush. Wet the whole sky and the mountains and drop the pinky-purple wash in above the horizon.

2 Paint the blue wash at the top of the sky, leaving white shapes for clouds. Scrub the brush dry on kitchen paper and use it to mop up runs, blend and manipulate the colour on the paper. Use a pad of kitchen paper to dry off excess water on the mountain so there will be no backruns.

3 Make two washes for the foreground gravel: dilute raw sienna and a thicker wash of raw sienna with neutral tint. Wet the area first with the no. 8 round, cutting round the boats, and put on the first wash.

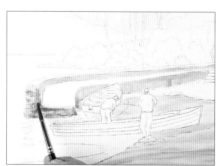

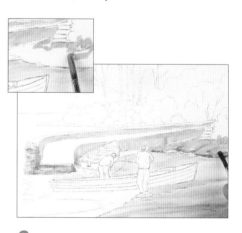

4 Bleed in strokes of the darker wash at an angle to show the contour of the ground. Nip the brush between your finger and thumb with kitchen paper to dry it and use it to blend and soften.

5 Paint the jetty with the same raw sienna wash, then bleed in a mix of raw sienna, neutral tint and cerulean blue to create texture.

6 Mix Winsor yellow and cobalt turquoise to paint the greenery at the bottom of the steps, then bleed in a thicker, darker wash of Winsor yellow and French ultramarine. Nip the brush dry and soften the dark wash in.

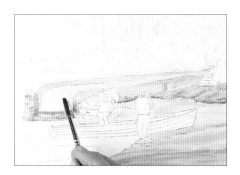

7 Use the first raw sienna wash to paint the sunlit walkway of the jetty.

8 Make four mountain washes with the 19mm (¾in) brush: four brushfuls of water with French ultramarine and a little light red; three brushfuls with Winsor yellow and French ultramarine; alizarin crimson and cerulean blue; and two brushfuls with French ultramarine and light red. Wet the area and paint the first wash in the direction of the fall.

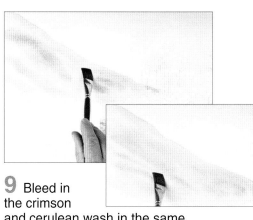

9 Bleed in the crimson and cerulean wash in the same direction. Nip the brush dry then bleed in the green wash from two-thirds of the way up. Dry the brush again and blend and soften.

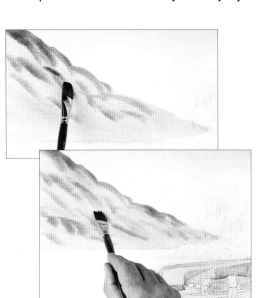

10 Bleed in the strong, dark wash of French ultramarine and light red with marks following the fall of the mountain, then dry the brush and use it to soften and blend.

11 Emphasise the texture with the no. 8 brush and the darkest wash, then use the 19mm (¾in) flat brush, dry, to pull the marks in little arcs, following the direction of the land.

12 Make washes for the bushes in the middle distance: three no. 8 brushfuls of water with Winsor yellow and Winsor blue; two brushfuls with Winsor yellow, lots of French ultramarine and a little light red. Paint a few non-adjacent bushes with the first wash.

13 Dot in the second wash, mainly on the left-hand sides and undersides, then the darker third wash on the extreme left-hand sides and undersides. Dry the brush and blend and diffuse the tones.

14 Mix a different green from Winsor blue and a very little raw sienna and paint this in another bush as the first wash, to vary the colours of the bushes. Bleed in and blend the subsequent washes as in steps 12 and 13. Paint other bushes in the same way.

15 Make three washes for the bank of trees behind the bushes: Winsor yellow and Winsor blue; Winsor yellow, French ultramarine and light red; and French ultramarine and light red. Paint on the first wash, cutting round the smaller trees. Dot in the second wash, making it thickest next to the nearer trees.

16 Paint the third, darkest wash down to the ground where the deep shadow is, painting negatively round the other trees.

17 Use a penknife to scratch out trunks and branches. Paint the field behind the bushes with the light Winsor yellow and Winsor blue wash, with the no. 8 brush, cutting round the tree trunks.

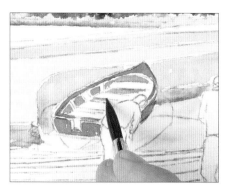

18 Paint the sand beneath the bushes with raw sienna and a little neutral tint, then shade the underside with French ultramarine and light red.

19 Make the wash for the red boat with a brushful of water, light red and Winsor red. Block in the body of the boat, leaving white edges where it catches the light.

20 Paint the larger boat with a mix of cobalt turquoise and cerulean blue, one plank at a time.

21 Use a dark mix of French ultramarine and light red to paint the dark shadows in the red boat and the interior and planking of the blue boat.

42

22 Paint the tree on the right with Winsor yellow, then dot in French ultramarine and Winsor yellow and let it bleed through. Bounce a dry brush over it to blend and soften, then when it is just damp, use a penknife to scratch out branches.

23 Block in the bush in front of this tree with Winsor yellow, then dot in the subsequent washes of French ultramarine and light red and blend as before.

24 Paint the grassy area between the bushes and gravel with Winsor yellow, then dot in a bit of the second wash.

25 Make a shadow mix from three brushfuls of water with French ultramarine, Winsor red and light red. Paint the inside of the jetty wall and its right-hand wall and intensify the shade with a thicker mix of the same colours where it curves. Bleed in this stronger wash.

26 To create stone texture on the darkest shadowed parts of the jetty, place kitchen paper over the area and rub a brush end through it.

27 Use the 19mm (¾in) flat brush to make a dilute wash of Winsor blue with a tiny bit of cerulean blue. Brush clean water on to the paper, then brush in the wash with horizontal lines, using the flat edge of the brush.

28 Scrub the brush dry and use it to smooth and blend the water, then brush in a stronger wash with more Winsor blue, in horizontal strokes.

29 Dry the brush and use it to pull the darker marks out to the left and blend them, then paint reflections under the boat and jetty with French ultramarine and light red. Feather out the reflections and strengthen them with a darker wash where needed.

30 Shade the side of the red boat, and add its cast shadow with French ultramarine, Winsor red and light red.

31 Paint the steps and the top of the jetty wall with dilute raw sienna.

32 Make horizontal marks of texture on the jetty walkway with raw sienna.

33 Mix raw sienna with neutral tint and paint the stones in the jetty wall.

34 Paint the wet sand behind the figures with the same mix.

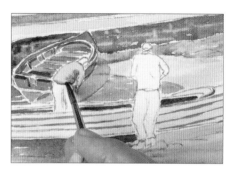

35 Block in the left-hand figure's top with a mix of cobalt turquoise and Winsor yellow, then bleed in French ultramarine and light red on the right-hand side to indicate shadows.

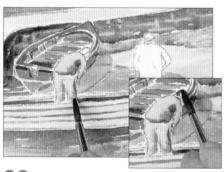

36 Block in the figure's trousers with dilute raw sienna, then bleed in shadow as in the previous step. Paint the hair with burnt sienna and neutral tint.

37 Paint the right-hand figure's top with Winsor red and light red, then bleed in shadow as before. Dry the brush and blend the shadow before it spreads too far.

38 Mix cerulean blue and light red to paint the figure's grey hair.

39 Paint the trousers with Winsor blue and Winsor yellow, then bleed in shadow with French ultramarine and light red. Allow to dry.

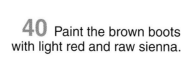

40 Paint the brown boots with light red and raw sienna.

41 Paint rocks on the beach with French ultramarine and light red, then use the same mix for the darks on the trousers.

42 Mix burnt sienna and neutral tint, then use the rigger to paint the silhouetted trunks of the background trees, painting up from the bottom and tapering the strokes to indicate the natural thinning of branches and twigs.

43 Paint the foliage with the no. 8 brush in a flat hold with a mix of raw sienna and Winsor blue, then modify and shape the blocks of foliage with the point of the brush.

44 Paint the foliage of the trees on the far right with a mix of Winsor yellow, French ultramarine and a little light red.

45 Mix burnt sienna and neutral tint and paint the distant fence with the rigger.

46 Redefine the base of the mountain at the water's edge with a mix of Winsor yellow, French ultramarine and light red. Dry the brush and blend this in so that it fades into the rest of the mountain.

47 Use the rigger and darks from the palette to add birds in the sky.

Overleaf

The finished painting.

45

DERMOT CAVANAGH.

Index

Cottage on Slieve Gullion Mountain, County Armagh.